SOME OPENING THOUGHTS...

A good friend and longtime professional colleague of mine named Ray Hunziker (who you may recognize as the chief editor of *Tropical Fish Hobbyist* magazine) referred to me the other day as an "occasional turtle-type." Barring the thought that this was some kind of herpetological insult, I took him to mean I am someone who occasionally indulges in the hobby

Leopard Geckos, Great Plains Skinks, and other such scuttling creatures that really only reach their peak of worldly usefulness when offered as snake food.

The point is, the people involved in the hobby of herptile-keeping seem to fall into specific categories, and these categories seem fairly easy to define. There are the turtle-types, the snake-types, the lizard-

Map turtles, genus *Graptemys*, have been part of the pet trade for a long time, but the Diamondback Terrapin, *Malaclemys terrapin* (which many experts consider to be a very close relative of the maps), is sort of a "newcomer" to the pet scene.

of turtle-keeping.

Having had the misfortune of putting up with me almost every day for the last four years, Ray has become somewhat familiar with my views on herpetoculture, and I have become familiar with his. He is one of those despicable "lizard-types," boasting a plump collection of

types, the frog and toad-types, and of course the salamander-types. Most fall into the snake and lizard categories, but turtle and amphibian fanatics are a strong and devoted band in their own right.

Having dabbled with turtles for some time, I've come to the

conclusion that the aquatic species are among the most interesting herptile pets you could ever keep. I've done books on both aquatic and terrestrial turtles (*Red-eared Sliders* and *Box Turtles*, both under the pseudonym of Jordan Patterson), and I have to confess I kind of prefer the former. Admittedly they are filthy creatures, but you accept that when you obtain one. It's all part of the aquatic-turtle craze. If you are, like me, a "turtle-type," then you will put

Diamondback Terrapins, on the other hand, have only recently captured the attention of the more discerning hobbyist. I found that out after I wrote an article for Ray's mag called "Diamondback Terrapins: Brackish Delights" (*Tropical Fish Hobbyist*; September, 1994; pgs. 89-98) and was barraged by a wave of enthusiastic phone calls and letters. "It was so nice to finally see an article about Diamondbacks! I've kept them for *years*, but I didn't think anyone

PHOTO BY K. T. NEMURAS.

Some map turtle species are more common in the herpetocultural hobby than others. This Barbour's Map, *Graptemys barbouri*, for example, is almost never seen in the pet trade except when offered by private breeders.

up with a little messiness in order to enjoy the privilege of keeping an animal that fascinates you.

Map turtles and Diamondback Terrapins fascinate a lot of people, myself included. I've always loved maps, and I know a lot of other people who do too. They've been sold through pet shops for years.

else did!" wrote one woman from Manhattan. I suspect her latter notion is shared by many Diamondback lovers.

That unexpected enthusiasm, plus the already proven enthusiasm for the maps, inspired this book. It's one more title in TFH's already massively successful "RE" series, and

PHOTO OF AN ALABAMA MAP, *GRAPTEMYS PULCHRA*, BY ISABELLE FRANCAIS.

The future keeper of maps and Diamondbacks must understand that these turtles are aquatic and therefore can be very demanding at times, especially in terms of housing. Most aquatic turtles, while intriguing, also can be very messy.

an attempt to further satisfy the small band of "turtle-types" who have an affection for the turtles of the genera *Graptemys* and *Malaclemys*. I've tried to cover all the little details concerning the keeping and breeding of these magnificent creatures, plus a little natural history, taxonomy, and identification. A complete picture is the target I was aiming for, and I hope I nailed it. Only you, the reader, can make that judgment for sure.

The ultimate goal, of course, is to make all your future experiences with map turtles and Diamondback Terrapins as rewarding as possible. If this book manages to do that, then I can ask no more.

W. P. Mara

DEDICATION

For reptiles and amphibians the world over, both here and gone, and for those yet to come. You were around long before us, yet we have the nerve to hold you in glass boxes and presume to be your masters.

Can you ever forgive us?

A BIT OF NATURAL HISTORY...

THE SPECIES AND THE SUBSPECIES

At present, there only is one Diamondback Terrapin species, while there are eleven map turtle species. The taxonomy of the map turtles has undergone a bit of shuffling in recent years, the two most notable changes being the addition of two new species from the southeastern United States and the reclassification of the Mississippi Map Turtle from a full species (*Graptemys kohni*) to a subspecies (of *G. pseudogeographica*). As for the Diamondbacks, there currently are seven subspecies in the group, and that status hasn't changed since 1955 when the last race was described.

GRAPTEMYS BARBOURI
BARBOUR'S MAP TURTLE
Carr and Marchand, 1942

Identification: The females of this species are considerably larger than the males—around 13 inches as compared to around five. The females also have larger and much broader heads that are almost grotesque in appearance. There is a yellow heart-shaped or Y-shaped pattern on the top of the head, plus a curved bar on the underside of the chin. Shell color is olive to an olive-brown with yellow, semilunar markings on the pleural scutes. The plastron is an off-white or yellowish white with there is some dark

Notice the Y-shaped mark surrounded by black on the head of this Barbour's Map Turtle, *Graptemys barbouri*. It is a characteristic of the species.

PHOTO BY R. D. BARTLETT

PHOTO BY W. P. MARA.

Described only in 1974, Cagle's Map Turtle, *Graptemys caglei*, is one of the most beautiful members of its genus. The ornate swirl-markings on the carapace are a distinguishing characteristic, as are the pale thin lines on the head and neck.

pigmentation along the transverse seams. The color of the skin is dark brown to black, and the markings are a light yellow to yellowish green. The stripes on the neck are wide and equal in size. There also is striping on the legs and tail.

Geography: Barbour's Map Turtle is found only in three states—Alabama, Georgia, and Florida—in the Apalachicola River and its related tributaries (Flint, Chipola, and Chattahoochee).

Subspecies: None.

GRAPTEMYS CAGLEI
CAGLE'S MAP TURTLE
Haynes and McKown, 1974

Identification: Males of this species grow to about 3.5 in/8.9 cm while the females reach about 6.5/16.5 cm. Color of the carapace is greenish to brown, each scute having yellowish, almost fingerprint-like markings. The legs and head are black with thin, pale yellowish linework. On the top of the head is a V-shaped mark, and there is a cream-colored, transverse bar on the chin. The plastron is cream-colored with a dark coloration enhancing the path of the seams.

Geography: The species is found only in south-central Texas, most specifically in the Gaudalupe/San Antonio River system. However, Vermersch, in 1992, stated that the species may be gone from the San Antonio sector.

Subspecies: None.

GRAPTEMYS ERNSTI
ESCAMBIA MAP TURTLE
Lovich and McCoy, 1992

Identification: This is a pretty good-sized turtle. Females grow to about 11.5 in/29 cm, and the males to about 5.25/13.3 cm. Carapace color is olive, and there is a well-defined broken dark stripe running down the center. There are yellow rings and vermiculations on the scutes, and the plastron is pale yellow with dark coloration enhancing the seams. The skin color is brown to olive and has light yellow or yellowish green striping or blotching. The striping on the neck is relatively thick. There is a large, light-colored blotch on the top of the head, and two more on either side (these not being connected to the one on the top). Some specimens have a light-colored blotch below each eye.

Geography: This species can be found only in southern Alabama and the Florida Panhandle, in rivers flowing into Pensacola Bay.

Subspecies: None.

GRAPTEMYS FLAVIMACULATA
YELLOW-BLOTCHED MAP TURTLE
Cagle, 1954

Identification: This is one of the smaller map turtles, males growing to about 4.4 in/11 cm and females to about 6.8 in/17 cm. Their heads are quite narrow and the edges of the marginal scutes are serrated. The shell is colored olive to brown, with a ring or yellow (or orangish) blotch on most scutes. Each of the scutes

One of the rarest and most beautiful map turtles is the Yellow-blotched Map, *Graptemys flavimaculata*, from Mississippi. It also is one of the smallest—the females (which are larger than the males) barely grow over half a foot.

The Common Map Turtle, *Graptemys geographica*, occurs over a fairly large area—from the Great Lakes region south almost to the Gulf Coast. It often turns up in the pet trade and does fairly well in captivity.

may have dark outlining. The plastron is very light, usually cream-colored, with the seams being more pronounced by a darkness that will fade in time. The skin is olive colored (sometimes fairly light) with a series of yellow stripes, those on the neck often counting out to 19.

Geography: *Flavimaculata* is found only in Mississippi, most specifically in the Pascagoula River and its major tributaries.

Subspecies: None.

GRAPTEMYS GEOGRAPHICA
COMMON MAP TURTLE
(LeSueur, 1817)

Identification: Females grow to a length of about 11/in/27.5 cm, the males to about 6.4 in/16 cm. The carapace is relatively low and there is a vague hint of knobbing only on juveniles and males; females have none whatsoever. There is a longitudinal yellow spot behind the eye. This animal gets its name from the intricate network of lines and swirls on its back, a pattern slightly reminiscent of a map. Lines and swirls are yellowish while the base color of the carapace is olive green. Skin color is brownish black, with the markings yellow or greenish yellow.

Geography: This species primarily is found around the Great Lakes region, but also extends southward almost to the

PHOTO BY R. D. BARTLETT.

The Pascagoula Map Turtle, *Graptemys gibbonsi*, is one of the most recently described maps. It wasn't so much "discovered" as it was taken from the existing species *Graptemys pulchra*. The reason for the "split" is because, geographically speaking, the *gibbonsi* population is isolated from the rest of *pulchra*.

Gulf Coast. Its westernmost state is Kansas (eastern area), it occurs south to central Alabama, east to southeastern New York and northwestern New Jersey (disjunct populations), and north to southern Quebec.

Subspecies: None

GRAPTEMYS GIBBONSI
PASCAGOULA MAP TURTLE
Lovich and McCoy, 1992

Identification: Females grow to about 11.8 in/29.5 cm, the males about half that. The shell is fairly high-domed for a map turtle, with a median keel and a vertical yellow bar on the dorsal surface of each marginal scute. The base color of the carapace is brownish olive, and there is a black medial stripe. On the pleural scutes are broad yellow rings and/or vermiculations. The skin is brown to brownish olive with stripes and/

or blotches that are light yellow to yellowish green. Interestingly, although the males have longer tails than the females, both sexes have relatively flat plastrons.

Geography: This species can be found only in the Pascagoula and Pearl rivers (in Mississippi and Louisiana) and their tributaries.

Subspecies: None

Graptemys gibbonsi can be found only in the Pascagoula and Pearl rivers, in Mississippi and Louisiana. Taxonomically, it was named after Dr. J. Whitfield Gibbons, who has devoted much of his life to the study of turtles, particularly in the eastern United States.

PHOTO BY R. D. BARTLETT.

GRAPTEMYS NIGRINODA
BLACK-KNOBBED MAP TURTLE
Cagle, 1954

Identification: Females grow to around 7.5 in/19.1 cm, the males to around 4.5 in/11.5 cm. Outstanding features include broadly knobbed spine tips (which are black) and narrow light rings on the carapace. Most specimens have a small, narrow head and a strongly serrated rim on the posterior of the carapace. The carapace is dark olive in color while the plastron is yellow, often with a red tinting and a black "branch" pattern. The skin is black with yellow stripes all around (head, limbs, neck, and tail). Two to four stripes on the neck enter the orbital region, and there are longitudinal yellow stripes on the low jaw that are as wide as the black interspaces.

PHOTO BY JORDAN PATTERSON.

By looking at this picture, you can get a pretty clear idea of how the Black-knobbed Map Turtle, *Graptemys nigrinoda*, got its name.

Notice the strongly serrated carapacial rim that is characteristic of the Black-knobbed Map Turtle. While other *Graptemys* species also have serrating, none have it as prominently as *nigrinoda*.

PHOTO BY JIM MERLI.

Geography: This species can be found only in Mississippi and Alabama, most specifically in the Tallapoosa, Coosa, Black Warrior, Tombigbee, and Cahaba river systems.

Subspecies: *G. n. delticola* (Delta Map Turtle); *G. n. nigrinoda* (Black-knobbed Map Turtle).

GRAPTEMYS OCULIFERA
RINGED MAP TURTLE
(Baur, 1890)

Identification: The females reach a length of around 8.5 in/21.6 cm, the males about 4 in/10.2 cm. This turtle can be distinguished by the broad rings on the dorsal scutes. Other characters include very conspicuous dorsal spines (Conant and Collins referred to this species as being among "the spiniest of our turtles"), light-colored mandibles, two broad stripes on the neck that enter the eye, and a large postorbital blotch. In the females, the rings on the scutes may be a little less obvious. On the juveniles, at the posterior area of the carapace, the marginal scutes may be quite pointed. The base color of the carapace is a medium to dark olive green, the distinctive rings being yellow or orange. The plastron is, like the rings, yellow or orange, with an olive-brown pattern following the seams. The basic color of the skin is black, and the striping is yellow.

Geography: Endemic to the Pearl River system (and its tributaries) in Mississippi and Louisiana.

Subspecies: None.

The Ringed Map Turtle, *Graptemys oculifera* (also known as the "Ringed Sawback") is one of the rarest turtles in the United States. It, along with the Yellow-blotched Map Turtle, is a federally protected species currently listed as "threatened."

PHOTO BY DR. P. C. H. PRITCHARD.

The False Map Turtle, *Graptemys pseudogeographica*, is one of the most commonly kept map turtles; thousands are sold every year. Shown is one of the lesser-seen subspecies, the Ouachita Map Turtle, *G. p. ouachitensis*.

GRAPTEMYS PSEUDOGEOGRAPHICA
FALSE MAP TURTLE
(Gray, 1831)

Identification: Females grow to around 10.75 in/27.3 cm, the males to a little over half that. Outstanding characteristics include a brown carapace (with brown or yellow oval markings and/or dark blotches on each pleural scute), a middorsal keel that is weakly knobbed at best, a very serrated posterior rim, and light spot or line directly behind the eye. Some of the light-colored lines on the neck reach the eye, but this character is not consistent enough to use for reliable identification.

The heads of both the males and females are relatively small compared to their bodies. The males, notably, have very long nails on their front feet.

Geography: This species is primarily native to the large streams of the Mississippi and Missouri rivers. It is known from Ohio, Indiana, Minnesota, Wisconsin, and North and South Dakota in the north, then moves south to Alabama, Mississippi, Louisiana, and Texas.

Subspecies: *G. p. ouachitensis* (Ouachita Map Turtle); *G. p. pseudogeographica* (False Map Turtle); *G. p. sabinensis* (Sabine Map Turtle).

PHOTO BY DR. P. C. H. PRITCHARD.

Notice the incredible size difference between this adult female Alabama Map Turtle, *Graptemys pulchra* (the larger one), and the adult male of the same species. Such a pronounced size difference between sexes is normal for the genus *Graptemys*.

GRAPTEMYS PULCHRA
ALABAMA MAP TURTLE
Baur, 1893

Identification: Adult females grow to about 11 in/27.9 cm, males to around 5 in/12.7 cm. The Alabama Map has a relatively low-domed carapace. Females, most notably, have revoltingly large heads in comparison to the rest of their body. Base color of the carapace usually is dark brown or dark olive with yellow outlining on the marginal scutes. Also present on each marginal is a yellow marking, usually in the shape of a ring. A black medial stripe can be seen following the keel, and this line often is broken up. The plastron is pale yellow, and dark pigmentation usually follows the seams. The skin color is, like the carapace, brown to olive, with light yellow or yellowish green stripes and/or blotches.

Geography: This species can be found only in the Mobile Bay drainage system in Alabama, Georgia, and perhaps Mississippi.

Subspecies: None.

GRAPTEMYS VERSA
TEXAS MAP TURTLE
Stejneger, 1925

Identification: This is one of the smaller map turtles. Females grow to a length of around 8 in/20.3 cm, and males grow to around 4.5 in/11.5 cm. There is a light yellow or orange line that runs back from the eye and often is J-shaped. There is a light-colored oval on the chin, near the point, and farther back on the chin, on either side, is a small round spot, also light in color. Towards the front of the carapace, many of the scutes are slightly "puffed;" an effect Conant and Collins described as "quilted." The head of this species is relatively small and narrow. The basic color of the carapace is olive and has yellow reticulations on each scute. There also is a vertebral keel with low and dark knobs, and the posterior portion of the marginals is strongly serrated. The plastron is yellow, and there is a darkening along the seams. The color of the skin is olive with yellow markings, and there are many dark lines surrounding the yellows.

Geography: The Texas Map can be found only in the Edwards Plateau in central Texas, more specifically in the Colorado River drainage.

Subspecies: None

MALACLEMYS TERRAPIN
DIAMONDBACK TERRAPIN
(Schoepff, 1793)

Identification: Females of this most attractive species grow to about 9 in/22.9 cm, and the males grow to about 5.5 in/14 cm. The male's head is fairly small, the female's is fairly large. One easy way to diagnose a Diamondback is to look for the concentric rings or ridges on the plastral scutes. Also, this species has heavily spotted skin (neck and limbs). Coloration of the carapace varies highly, often depending on the subspecies, often depending on locality. Generally speaking, the carapace can be light gray, light brown, dark olive, dark brown, and even black. From there, patterns either can be nonexistent or consist of

The Texas Map Turtle, *Graptemys versa*, has an interesting diagnostic characteristic—it has a reddish or orange stripe behind the eye. Because of this, it could very easily be mistaken for the ubiquitous Red-eared Slider, *Trachemys scripta elegans*, from a distance.

many lines that follow the concentric rings or ridges and are lighter than the ground color. Plastron usually is orange to yellow gray or greenish gray and can be either marked or unmarked. Often there is a gray 'hazing' and a series of medium to dark gray speckles. Sometimes you will see dark markings on the upper jaw, creating a 'mustache' effect. The hind feet are very large, and both front and hind feet are conspicuously webbed.

Geography: A creature of brackish water, it can be found along the Atlantic and Gulf coasts, from Cape Cod to Texas. It is native to the Florida Keys but does not occur in Mexico.

Subspecies: *M. t. centrata* (Carolina Diamondback Terrapin); *M. t. littoralis* (Texas Diamondback Terrapin); *M. t. macrospilota* (Ornate Diamondback Terrapin); *M. t. pileata* (Mississippi Diamondback Terrapin); *M. t. rhizophorarum* (Mangrove Diamondback Terrapin); *M. t. tequesta* (Florida East Coast Terrapin); *M. t. terrapin* (Northern Diamondback Terrapin).

HABITAT

The map turtles have been

Undoubtedly one of the most beautiful Diamondback Terrapin subspecies, the Ornate Diamondback, *Malaclemys terrapin macrospilota*, occasionally turns up in pet shops. It is a hardy captive with a voracious appetite, and it can be bred with relative ease.

PHOTO BY JIM MERLI.

Plastron of the Ornate Diamondback Terrapin, *Malaclemys terrapin macrospilota*. Most Diamondbacks have relatively simple plastral colors and patterns.

PHOTO BY MELLA PANZELLA.

The Diamondback Terrapin is the only truly brackish-water turtle in the world. There are other turtles that spend time in brackish-water habitats, but only the Diamondback can claim these places as their "full-time" home. Particular areas include tidal creeks, salt marshes, and ocean estuaries.

aptly described as "lake and river dwellers," where they will spend a good portion of their day resting on the exposed parts of half-submerged logs and soaking in sunlight. Specific reported habitats include limestone-based streams and rivers, mud-bottomed streams with a gentle current, sand- and gravel-based creeks and rivers with a relatively rapid flow, and wide rivers with sand bars (that are used for both basking and nesting) and a preponderance of snags, brush, and debris.

The Diamondback Terrapin is perhaps the only turtle in the world that can claim bodies of brackish water as its main habitat. While many turtles

Map turtles often are referred to as "lake and river dwellers." Frequented areas include limestone-based streams and rivers, sand-and gravel-based creeks, and broad rivers with sandbars (which often are used as egglaying sites). Waters are both slow- and and fast-moving.

Newborn Diamondback Terrapins are almost impossible to find in the wild. Their secretive nature, however, is one of their defense mechanisms—since they are so susceptible to predators, they have no choice but to remain *in cognito* most of the time. Shown is a hatchling Northern Diamondback, *Malaclemys terrapin terrapin*.

PHOTO BY K. T. NEMURAS.

venture into brackish water every now and then, only the Diamondback spends the vast majority of its time there. Specific habitats include coastal salt marshes and estuaries, and tidal creeks.

HABITS

In the wild, map turtles are devotedly diurnal and spend much of their time out of the water, basking on whatever familiar sites are available. Interestingly, maps usually use only well-established sites, meaning those that have been used for generations, rather than those that have recently appeared, like logs or trees that have recently fallen. It is worth noting that most maps avoid basking sites that are relatively close to shorelines, preferring the safety of those that are in deep water and are a good distance from land. They will actively and purposely search for the highest spot available, presumably so they'll be able to spot potential predators as early as possible. Maps are remarkably nervous and alert and will dive off their basking spot at the first hint of danger.

The Diamondback Terrapin is a little bit calmer than the

Unlike most map turtles, the Diamondback Terrapin is a relatively calm creature that will allow most observers to come within reasonable proximity. Of course, no specimen would ever allow you to walk up and touch it!

PHOTO OF A MANGROVE DIAMONDBACK TERRAPIN, MALACLEMYS TERRAPIN RHIZOPHORARUM, BY K. H. SWITAK.

Map turtles are incredibly nervous, diving from their basking sites at the first sign of danger. This makes them nearly impossible to catch, which is good news for the turtles but bad for the scientists who need to study them. Shown is an Alabama Map Turtle, *Graptemys pulchra*.

average map turtle, basking along the muddy shores of its brackish water bodies. It can be observed from a reasonable distance but will not allow you within capturing proximity. It too is decidedly diurnal, although gravid females may become crepuscular or nocturnal. The Diamondback often spends its nights buried in mud, presumably as a safety measure against predation.

As far as feeding in the wild is concerned, both maps and the Diamondback Terrapin seem to accept a broad variety of items. Maps are particularly amenable to different things. Recorded items include snails, clams, mussels, fish, many different types of insects and insect larvae, shrimp, crayfish, millipedes, centipedes, spiders, and earthworms. Interestingly, a great deal of plant material has been found during stomach-content studies of various map turtles; one specimen even had traces of tree bark. However, it is generally believed that these herbivore items found their way into the turtles' stomachs simply because they were swallowed during the capture of the turtles' normal prey. Also notable is the fact that many studies have shown a sex/diet preference, e.g., females often have a different diet than males.

The Diamondback Terrapin, like any other animal, eats what it can find in its natural habitat. Since the Terrapin is a creature of brackish water bodies and their surrounding area, it has developed a preference for things like various gastropods (including periwinkles), crabs, shrimp, certain small bivalves (including blue mussels), annelids, clams, various fishes (both alive and dead), and some plant material. Interestingly, neonates seem more willing to try different things than adults, as was concluded by a lab study where newborns ate virtually anything, then, by the end of their first year, began to steadfastly refuse items they were willing to accept only a few months before. Other items taken by lab-kept specimens include various store-bought shellfish, snails, beef, liver, salmon, tuna, cooked and chilled shrimp, and freeze-dried shrimp.

Since Diamondback Terrapins are creatures of brackish-water surroundings, their diet consists of items such as crabs, shrimp, clams, and various gastropods. A keeper may find these items difficult to acquire, but most captive Diamondbacks will accept more obtainable things after a short "weaning" period. Shown is a Mississippi Diamondback Terrapin, *Malaclemys terrapin pileata*.

HOUSING

The task of properly housing of an aquatic turtle can easily turn into a nightmare, especially if you're the type of keeper who really doesn't have a lot of spare time. Truly efficient housing for map turtles and Diamondback Terrapins demands constant attention to cleanliness, and cleanliness means labor. Let's face it—aquatic turtles are filthy creatures. They have a great gift for defecating in their water (usually just after you've changed it), which means their enclosures will need sanitation attention every day.

However, a true enthusiast will not find any of this discouraging. Instead, he or she simply will accept it as a part of The Almighty Challenge, viewing cleaning chores as a labor of love rather than a demand of necessity.

SIZE OF THE ENCLOSURE

Map turtles and Diamondback Terrapins grow to a pretty

Housing aquatic turtles can be a real chore, especially in terms of keeping them clean. Most, like this Black-knobbed Map Turtle, *Graptemys nigrinoda*, have an annoying habit of defecating in their water right after it's been changed.

PHOTO BY R. D. BARTLETT.

respectable size. The size of the tank you choose obviously will depend on the size of your turtles plus the number of specimens you're keeping. For the sake of simplicity, we'll assume you're keeping a pair because eventually you'll want to breed them. Using this as the base reference and assuming further that you will be housing specimens in an all-glass aquarium (which is best), the ideal tank sizes are as follows—

CREATING THE HALF-LAND/HALF-WATER SETUP

Since the turtles discussed in this book are highly aquatic, they are going to need a large water body in which to swim around. However, they also are baskers (map turtles more so than Diamondbacks), so they will require an area of land as well.

The type of setup required is sometimes called an *aquaterrarium* or a *paludarium*,

SHELL LENGTH	SIZE OF AQUARIUM
up to 2 inches.....................	10 gallon standard
2 to 3 inches	20 gallon long
3 to 4 inches	30 gallon long
4 to 5 inches	40 gallon standard
5 to 7 inches	55 gallon standard
over 7 inches	Turtles are best kept in an outdoor pond.

Outdoor enclosures are a slice of heaven for captive turtles. And, in many ways, they are beneficial to a keeper as well. For one thing, the full-spectrum lighting is already provided. Also, an efficiently filtered pond basically cleans itself.

A simple way of creating a half-land/half-water setup is by affixing a clear plastic pane on a 45° angle from the floor up, as shown here.

but whatever the name, the basic concept is an enclosure made up of both land and water. On the most basic level, such a setup can be provided simply by half-filling a glass tank and placing in a few rockpiles or logs that rise above the water level. More intensely, you can divide the tank into two separate sections with the aid of a pane of clear plastic and some silicone sealant. One side can be strictly for water, the other filled with soil or gravel and attractively decorated with plants, rocks, and so on. Of course, the latter setup will require a bit more effort on your part, but with time and patience you can create a very beautiful display.

The real point here is that map turtles and Diamondback Terrapins not only like to bask, they *need* to bask, so the provision of some sort of dry area is a *must* (particularly with neonates, who will drown if not given a place to sit and rest).

THE NEVER-ENDING "BRACKISH WATER DEBATE"

Virtually every person I have ever spoken with concerning the keeping of Diamondback Terrapins has asked me the same question—'Do they need to be kept in brackish water in captivity?'

When you're ready to set up your first aquaterrarium, your local pet shop should be able to provide you with a "starter kit" of some kind. Most starter kits will, at the very least, have all the basic filtration components. Photo courtesy of Penn Plax.

The answer, honestly, is no. I have read fist-hammering reports on both sides of this issue—claims that Diamondbacks kept in freshwater tanks develop severe shell fungus, shell deformities, loss of appetite, etc. On the other hand, I could show you published citations of Diamondbacks being kept in the same freshwater setups with other aquatic turtles and developing no problems whatsoever.

I am speaking from experience here. I have kept many Diamondback Terrapins in freshwater enclosures, and *never once* did any of my specimens develop fungus, deformities, or any of the other mythical ailments. At one time I did try to replicate a brackish water body—a half-teaspoon of kosher salt per gallon of water. But then I decided to start using water right from my tap, and lo and behold, no crises arose. Of course, I should point out that every time I did a water change I also gave all my turtles a "bath," not only soaking them but also using a very soft sponge to scrub their shells. Fungus never even had the *chance* to form.

The choice, of course, is yours. You certainly won't be doing any harm to a Diamondback if you put it in a brackish water setup. But, in my experience, you also won't be doing them any harm if you don't, either.

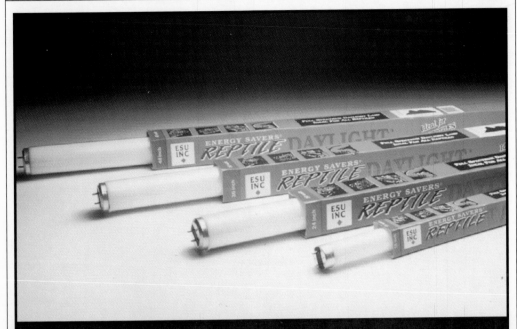

Full-spectrum lighting is essential in conjunction with the keeping of aquatic turtles. Such lights can be purchased at most pet shops that stock herpetocultural goods. Photo courtesy of Energy Savers.

Map turtles and Diamondback Terrapins that are denied exposure to full-spectrum lighting may live in captivity for a short time, but in the long run they probably will develop softshell disease, which, once started, is very difficult to reverse. Shown is a Florida East Coast Diamondback Terrapin, *Malaclemys terrapin tequesta*.

PHOTO BY AARON NORMAN.

LIGHTING

As any experienced turtle keeper will tell you, turtles of all kinds, whether they be land or water turtles, require not just any type of light, but a very special kind known as *full-spectrum* light. In short, full-spectrum light replicates that which is given off by the sun. For turtles, it is essential that such light be provided, because direct contact with it plays a major role in proper bone growth and shell development. Without it, a turtle will suffer a serious calcium deficiency and may die.

It should be noted that some keepers prefer to ignore the provision of full-spectrum light and instead give their turtles calcium through dietary supplements. However, it probably is best to offer at least some full-spectrum lighting even if you are giving such supplements.

A full-spectrum bulb can be purchased at any pet shop that carries herpetocultural goods, but be prepared—such bulbs are fairly expensive. Most are of the long tubular variety (fluorescent) and come in a few different of sizes. The bulb should be suspended above the enclosure so the rays will reach the turtles directly; rays aimed through glass walls will be filtered of their beneficial qualities (which is why you can't simply park the enclosure next to a sunlit window).

Aside from being given full-spectrum light, maps and Diamondbacks also should be

Newborn maps and Diamondbacks are particularly susceptible to softshell disease, so full-spectrum lighting *must* be given to them, especially during their first two years. Softshell disease in a neonatal aquatic turtle acts quickly and almost always proves fatal. Photo of a Northern Diamondback Terrapin, *Malaclemys terrapin terrapin*, by Mella Panzella.

exposed to ordinary light. A photoperiod (day/night cycle) of about 12 hours of light per day is recommended, so you'll need some sort of harmless supplementary light to use when the full-spectrum bulb is off. Overall, I would say a 4- to 6-hour exposure of full-spectrum light within a 12-hour exposure to ordinary light is perfect for the turtles discussed here.

HEATING

Turtles, like all other reptiles, are cold-blooded and thus rely on their environmental temperature for bodily warmth. In captivity, the keeper must provide this. If a turtle is allowed to become too cold, it may 1) have such a slow metabolism that it won't eat, 2) slip into premature hibernation, and/or 3) die.

Fortunately, providing heat in an aquatic turtle's setup is not a difficult undertaking. In a half-land/half-water setup, you can heat either the water, the land, or both.

With the water, the best method is the use of something called a *fully submersible heater.* Such heaters basically are as long glass tubes with a heating element inside and a heavily coated wire that runs off the

Keeping an eye on the ambient temperature and humidity of your turtle's enclosure is an important facet of good husbandry. If the animal is allowed to become too warm or too dry, it could become ill. Fortunately, both thermometers and hygrometers have been designed specifically for the needs of herptile keepers. Photo courtesy of Ocean Nutrition.

end and terminates in an ordinary household plug. There also should be some sort of thermostat control. Most pet shops that carry fish-keeping goods will have fully submersible heaters. They range in size and power and usually are very affordable.

Along with the heater should be a small bracket with suction cups that attaches right to the glass wall of the aquarium. Once attached, you simply slip the heater into the brackets. Always make sure the heater is completely submerged. If it isn't, it may overheat and crack, then the electricity can run through the water and fry your shelled friends. Also, make sure the thermostat is set at a reasonable level before putting in the turtles. The water temperature shouldn't go over 80°F/26°C, and ideally it should be closer to 75°F/24°C.

Finally, after a time, you may notice a rock-like buildup on the glass of the heater. As best as I can tell, this develops from a turtle's habit of resting directly under the heater with its shell pressed against it, so I guess it's some sort of shell by-

PHOTO BY W. P. MARA.

Keep in mind that any aquatic turtle kept in a cold environment probably will not eat. The ideal temperature for maps and Diamondbacks is around 82°F/28°C. Shown is a Northern Diamondback Terrapin, *Malaclemys terrapin terrapin*.

product. Regardless of what it is, I have found it nearly impossible to remove, so the best thing I can tell you to do is just ignore it. It doesn't seem to do any harm to the turtles or the heater, so it really should be of no concern.

As far as heating the land mass is concerned, the best way to do this is by providing something called a *spot lamp*. In short, a spot lamp is just what it sounds like—a lamp that heats one particular spot. Spot lamps also can be found at pet shops that have a lot of herpetocultural goods, and special heat-producing bulbs should be found in the same place. Keep a spot lamp high

enough above an enclosure so the turtles don't get burned, and remember to turn it off during the night.

In the case of aquatic turtles, it is ideal for you to choose a basking area for them and then heat only that. If you heat the *entire* enclosure, you are denying the turtles a cooler area to go to if they feel *too* warm. Basking sites should be large enough to fit all the turtles in the enclosure and should be very sturdy. An ideal air temperature for a map turtle's or Diamondback Terrapin's enclosure is around 82°F/28°C. (Above 85°F/29°C is too hot.)

The stronger the filter, the less you'll have to change the water in the enclosure. Your local pet shop should carry a wide range of filters to accommodate a wide range of tank setups. Photo courtesy of Penn Plax.

FILTRATION

As any fishkeeper will tell you, the process of keeping tank water clean can sometimes be problematical to say the least. Making it *look* clean is not enough; it actually has to *be* clean. With fishes, this can be difficult, but with aquatic turtles, it often is nearly impossible. Why? Because virtually all aquatic turtles are, in a sense, shameless slobs. Here's a question you can pitch to someone who has already had extensive experience with aquatic turtles—'Does it ever seem like your turtles only want to defecate immediately after you've changed their water?' A second question, along slightly similar lines, might be 'Do you ever feel like you never can *keep* the water clean for very long?'

The bottom line, again, is that aquatic turtles, like it or not, are filthy creatures, so filtration is an absolute necessity. What degree of filtration you decide on will be based largely on how much time you have to perform complete water changes. With a complicated and elaborate filtration setup, you may have to change the water only once a month. With a simpler filter arrangement, it may be once a week. In either case, water changes have to be made at some time or another. There's no avoiding them.

Using a box filter (often referred to as a "bubble" filter) is the simplest way to provide tank filtration. I say simplest because box filters are inexpensive and easy to set up. These are the box-shaped items you see tucked in the corner of virtually every 10-gallon pet-store fish tank. There'll be a line of plastic tubing running from the top of the filter to an external pump (usually a "bladder" pump) that forces air into the filter, thus creating a flow of water through the filter's charcoal and cotton-floss medium, which in turn traps a great deal of the filth in the tank.

On a more advanced level, external canister filters are very effective in spite of the fact that some can be very expensive.

These are, as the name implies, cylindrical in shape, and they operate via tubes running in and out of the water. One of the great conveniences is that you can change the filter medium without having to stick your hands into the tank water. Also, most canister filters are very quiet.

Finally, undergravel filters are popular with many keepers. The main advantage to these is that they remove a lot of the bulk filth, i.e., large feces, uneaten foodstuffs, etc. The disadvantage is that they usually don't work well with *biological* cleaning. They may take a lot of the junk off the tank floor, but the water usually remains pretty dirty. Combined with a box filter, an undergravel model works well. Still, if you have only a few turtles and commit yourself to regular water changes, undergravel filters are perfectly acceptable.

When housing many aquatic turtles, you may want to consider using *two* filters—one for the conspicuous junk in the water (the stuff you can see), and the other for the biological junk (the stuff you can't see). Turtles like this Black-knobbed Map Turtle, *Graptemys nigrinoda*, will quickly become ill if left in water that looks clean but in fact is loaded with pathogens.

PHOTO BY W. P. MARA

FEEDING

Keepers rarely need to worry when it comes to the feeding of map turtles and Diamondback Terrapins. From the outset, most specimens will be hardy and voracious. Some have an innate stubbornness when subjected to the confines of captivity, but in time even these animals will calm down and begin eating regularly

Good husbandry is, of course, directly related to an animal's willingness (or unwillingness) to eat. A turtle that wants to eat everything in sight will lose its appetite if it's ill or kept in a filthy enclosure. Providing the correct environment is very important for the stimulation of a feeding response, so be sure you house your turtles just right.

FOOD ITEMS

There are many items a captive map turtle or Diamondback Terrapin can be offered. I will list most of the common ones here, describing what they are and how you can go about getting them. If your own particular pet is offered every single item on this list and still does not eat, then you can pretty much assume there is a genuine problem to be dealt with, either in regards to the animal's health, or concerning the quality of its captive care.

Earthworms

The earthworm is one of the most common turtle food items, especially in the wild. An

It may be a while before wild-caught maps and Diamondbacks fully adjust to captive life. During this period, they may only want food items found in their natural habitat (which sometimes can be very difficult to obtain, especially in the case of the Diamondbacks).

PHOTO BY W. P. MARA.

Most maps and Diamondbacks will accept crickets right from the start. The great thing about crickets is that they are offered by most pet shops and are relatively inexpensive. They also are very nutritious.

earthworm provides many animals with a good deal of nutrition (although earthworms should not be offered as a staple food).

Earthworms can be harvested in your backyard by placing sheets of fabric over wet leaves, then waiting a day or two for the worms to come up. Another approach is to get in touch with a fisherman's bait shop and purchase worms in quantity. Earthworms can be frozen and thawed for later use, but remember to wrap them individually or else they'll stick together and you'll end up with one large disgusting "worm mass."

Crickets

Perhaps the most popular of all turtle livefoods is the cricket. Crickets are relished by map turtles and Diamondback Terrapins alike and provide them with plenty of nutrition.

Crickets of various sizes can be purchased in quantity at your local pet shop, or they can be ordered in bulk quantities from a few breeders (yes, there are professional cricket breeders). Of course, for the average keeper, the first choice is better because you only have to buy what you need at the moment. A pet store will gladly sell you ten crickets, but a breeder usually only sells in quantities of 500 or more. That means you not only will have to care for your turtles, but for their food as well.

Mealworms and Waxworms

Both items are greatly desired by most aquatic turtles, and both can purchased in quantity at pet shops. Mealworms are the larval form of the flour beetle, *Tenebrio*

PHOTO BY W. P. MARA.

Depending on where you live, you may be able to travel within a reasonable distance to collect livefood items for your map turtles and Diamondback Terrapins. Crayfish, for example, often can be found under large stones in streambeds.

Freeze-dried mealworms can be purchased at many pet shops. They offer a keeper the convenience of being able to feed his or her turtles right from a jar. Photo courtesy of Fluker Farms.

molitor, and can be offered as a supplementary food. Waxworms also should be given only in supplement because they are a little too fatty to be offered constantly.

If you wish to maintain a colony of mealworms, you can do it quite easily by filling a fairly large plastic container (such as a plastic sweaterbox) with oatmeal,

then dump in about 200 adult mealworms. Keep it in a cool and dark place and make sure there are a few small holes in the lid for ventilation (not too many, but a few). In time, the worms will transform into black, hard-shelled adults. The turnover rate runs in intervals of a few months, so it is advised that once you get one colony going really well, you start a few more. That way, you will assure yourself a continual mealworm flow.

"Seafood"

Fish, snails, mussels, shrimp, clams, etc.—these are items that most maps and Diamondback Terrapins should take without a fuss. I mention such items because many specimens, particularly those that are fresh from the wild, may not want anything else. I once had a beautiful neonatal Northern Diamondback Terrapin that refused all foods except raw shrimp for the first six months in

Above: Mealworms are a wonderful supplementary food item for aquatic turtles, but since they are not nutritionally complete, they should not be used as a staple item. **Below:** Fairy shrimp, like crayfish, can be found at most pet shops and are a highly nutritious supplementary item for maps and Diamondbacks.

Farm-raised crayfish can be purchased at many pet shops and are a wonderful "treat" item for map turtles and Diamondback Terrapins. Note, however, that they should be considerably smaller than the turtles they're being fed to. Large specimens will be able to put up a good fight and may injure your turtles in the process.

PHOTO BY M. P. AND C. PIEDNOIR.

captivity. I offered commercial food sticks, crickets, worms, and all the other standard goodies, but only shrimp solicited a feeding response. Finally, the animal began taking crickets, and, two months after that, it accepted its first "stick from a can."

The two main disadvantages to offering seafood items are 1) most will make the tank water very dirty (greasy), and 2) some are difficult to acquire. To solve the first problem, you'll just have to change the tank water more often. To solve the second, you'll either have to find a supermarket that sells seafood at a reasonable price, make friends with a fisherman, get in touch with a seafood market, or, if you live near the shore, buy some wading boots and a fishing pole, a minnow trap, and a clam rake.

Fruits and Vegetables

There's no doubting the nutritional value of fruits and vegetables. We eat them because they're good for us, so why not give some to our map turtles and Diamondback Terrapins?

Truth be told, maps and Diamondbacks are not very herbivorous, but again, once an aquatic turtle gets used to being in captivity it'll eat pretty much anything. I can't tell you how many Diamondback Terrapins I've kept that have eaten pieces of apple and banana. Diamondbacks in particular seem to go into a sort of hypnotic feeding frenzy, during which time they probably would chew the chrome off a bumper hitch.

I'm not going to get into a long discussion over which fruits and vegetables are ideal. The bottom

Snails usually are accepted with great eagerness by both maps and Diamondback Terrapins. A keeper should make a point of occasionally offering hard-shelled items like these so their turtles don't develop overgrown mandibles.

PHOTO BY KEN LUCAS.

PHOTO BY PAUL FREED.

Map turtles and Diamondback Terrapins should accept most insects without too much fuss, especially after they've grown accustomed to captive living. Many different types of insects can be collected in woods and overgrown meadows, but make sure you avoid areas that have been treated with pesticides.

line is, most of them are. There are some exceptions, of course— iceberg lettuce, for example, is nutritionally valueless. If you know about nutrition, then you'll have no problem finding the best choices. If not, consult a nutrition guide or talk to someone who has an interest in good dietary habits. As with so many other items discussed in this chapter, fruits and vegetables shouldn't be offered as a staple food, but as a supplement. Remember to chop them into bite-sized pieces, and don't be discouraged if your turtles won't accept them. Like I said

before, maps and Diamondbacks aren't really herbivores.

Strips of Raw Meat

I know many keepers who insist their turtles eagerly accept strips of raw meat. I've never tried this myself, but again, after a turtle gets used to being in captivity it will eat just about anything. Apparently, maps and Diamondbacks will accept a variety of meats, including liver, beef, beef heart, chicken, turkey, pork, and even veal.

The important things to remember here is that meat with a high fat content is bad, so only

PHOTO BY MICHAEL GILROY.

Once mealworms mature, they become hard-shelled black beetles. At this stage, they are highly nutritious and can be offered as a staple food item. Chances are, however, you'll want to keep the adults in order to support captive-raised pupae cultures.

offer meat that is very lean. Also, raw meat should be offered only as a supplement, not a staple. Give it in portions that are small enough for the animals to swallow whole, and use forceps so you don't lose any fingers. The bite of a large map turtle or Diamondback Terrapin will be felt for days.

Collected "Bugs"

Since you now know that map turtles and Diamondback Terrapins love insects and other assorted "bugs," you are probably wondering why you can't just go out into your own backyard or local woodland and get some. Well, you can, but have to be careful about it. Farm fields are a bad location because they often have been treated with pesticides.

Once you've located an area that you know to be safe, go there with a sweep net (like a butterfly net) and run it across the tall grasses and over the tops of shrubs and so forth, then transfer your catches to a jar, bring them home, and dump them into the tank. Don't capture too much at once unless you plan to set up a holding enclosure. Simply dumping a load of wild-caught bugs into the turtle tank may spoil the environment of that setup because any bugs that don't get eaten will die and rot.

PHOTOS BY MICHAEL GILROY (TOP) AND MARK SMITH (BOTTOM).

Tubifex worms are an excellent dietary item for map turtles and Diamondback Terrapins, especially neonatal specimens of the latter. They can be purchased both live or frozen in most pet shops that carry fish supplies (many fish eat them as well).

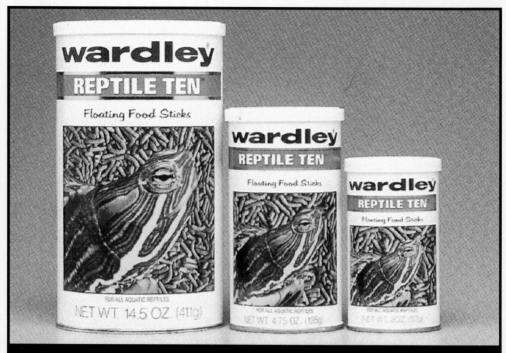

Commercially produced turtle foods, which usually come in either pellet or stick form, are sold at many pet shops. Most are specially blended to provide an aquatic turtle with all its nutritional needs. Photo courtesy of Wardley.

Bloodworms and *Tubifex* Worms

Both of these items can be purchased at pet shops in quantity and will be appreciated by younger map turtle and Diamondback Terrapin specimens. *Tubifex* is the name of the worm's genus but is also its commercial name. Both *Tubifex* and bloodworms can be purchased either frozen or live, the latter being the more preferable because the turtles seem to respond better to worms when they are alive and moving about.

Commercially Produced Foods

Most pet shops offer a selection of canned turtle foods, these being either rod-shaped or pellet-shaped. Such foods can be purchased in quantity and have been designed to meet virtually all of a turtles' nutritional needs.

Some turtles refuse canned foods, but only at the beginning of their term in captivity. It has been my experience that virtually all aquatic turtles kept in captivity for over six months *at the longest* will accept floating food sticks or food pellets.

Using commercial turtle food offers a great number of conveniences for the keeper. For example, 1) you can find commercial foods in most pet shops that carry herptile goods, 2) most commercial foods are inexpensive, and 3) most can be used as a staple diet. Also, commercial foods don't seem to make the tank water as messy as do many other food items.

Vitamin Additives

Every captive animal, no matter what it may be, should be given a regular dosage of vitamin supplements. With map turtles and Diamondback Terrapins, this usually is offered via the food items that have been either sprinkled with vitamin powder or "gut-loaded," which, in essence, means the food items have been fed a great deal of vitamins, which then are passed to the animal that eats them. Check with your local pet shop to see what type of vitamins they offer. Sprinkle them on the foods before offering (once every two weeks), or add them into the diet of your turtles' livefoods.

A word of caution—resist the urge to over-vitaminize your turtles. This is easier to do than you might imagine. Giving a turtles a lot of vitamins will not make them healthier, it will kill them instead through something known as hypervitaminosis. Remember, once every two weeks is fine.

HOW MUCH, HOW OFTEN?

A common question among beginning turtle keepers is "How much food should I give my turtles and how often?" In truth, this really isn't too tough to answer—use your own judgment. Each of your pets needs to be evaluated individually. The key is, don't overstuff them, but rather give them just enough to keep them satisfied, but still a little hungry so they'll be eager for the next feeding. Overfeeding, it should be noted, is very

Powdered calcium supplements can be purchased at most pet shops that carry other herpetocultural goods. Such powders should be sprinkled on a turtle's food (in conservative amounts) at least once a week. Photo courtesy of American Reptile.

PHOTO OF A FALSE MAP TURTLE, *GRAPTEMYS PSEUDOGEOGRAPHICA*, BY K. T. NEMURAS.

Adult map turtles and Diamondback Terrapins should be fed at least every two to three days. Younger specimens can feed every day, although the amounts should be relatively small.

dangerous. Not only does it produce obese animals that won't be able to move, they also won't be able to breed and may even die.

As far as scheduling is concerned, I feed my turtles every three to four days. This, of course, can also vary depending on the general rule that younger specimens need to eat more often than adults. For your average adult map turtle or Diamondback Terrapin, I'd say again that every three or four days is good, and for younger ones, every other day or third day.

beautifully and lovingly arranged setup, then sink into a state of depression and discouragement because the animal won't eat.

Assuming the turtle is not sick (and if you read through this section, following the advice, and the turtle *still* doesn't eat, then maybe it *is* sick), chances are you simply have a turtle that wants more "naturalistic" food items, i.e., items it was eating before someone came along and stuffed it in a sack.

If you end up with a turtle that

PHOTO BY W. P. MARA.

One reason captive-bred newborn map turtles and Diamondback Terrapins, like this Mississippi Map Turtle, *Graptemys pseudogeographica kohni*, are more desirable than wild-caught specimens is because they rarely put up a fuss when it comes to feeding. Unfortunately, the keeper has to be careful not to *over*feed them, which is very easy to do considering how voracious they usually are.

FEEDING PROBLEMS

More than once in this chapter I talked about turtles that need to "adjust" to life in captivity before they will accept certain food items. This is a common problem with aquatic turtles. Often a keeper will get his or her new purchase home, place it in a

seems to fit this description, the best approach to take is simply to give it what it wants. Think the problem out logically—what would this animal be eating if it were still in the wild? Answers will float to the surface if you think from this angle. A lot of the natural history information I've given you

If you have a map turtle or Diamondback Terrapin that won't eat even after you've tried all the prescribed "tricks," you probably should take it to a vet. Internal parasitic infestations, for example, are a common cause of feeding problems. Shown is a Mississippi Map Turtle, *Graptemys pseudogeographica kohni*.

will help; if you're stuck for ideas, go back to that chapter and read through the section on what maps and Diamondbacks eat in the wild. Read through other references sources as well. There only are so many items a map turtle or Diamondback Terrapin will eat.

Once you discover the correct item, keep giving it, in quantity, but slip in some other items at the same time. I once had a Mississippi Map Turtle that refused everything but live crickets. After she'd been in captivity for about a month, I started including a few commercial food sticks along with each handful of crickets. At first she didn't seem interested, but eventually she decided to get crazy and give one a try. Two months later, after a gradual decrease in crickets and an increase in sticks, she was on a mostly commercial-food diet.

Feeding problems should be taken care of as soon as possible. Captive map turtles and Diamondback Terrapins that don't eat will whither away to nothing in a remarkably short time.

CAPTIVE BREEDING

Anyone who keeps adult pairs of *any* herptile species has a responsibility to at least take a shot at breeding them. In this age of wholesale habitat destruction and large-scale collecting, anyone who claims to be a "lover" of their pets should do all they can to preserve their animals, and propagating them certainly is a part of that.

Breeding aquatic turtles is not as difficult as one might think. Yes, a modicum time and attention to detail is required, but that applies to the proper execution of any task. Perhaps the most difficult aspect of breeding map turtles and Diamondback Terrapins is the space requirements. You need a lot of room for them to both hibernate and copulate, but not so much that a truly dedicated enthusiast won't be able to provide it.

CHOICE OF SPECIMENS

The first step in any breeding cycle is the choosing of viable specimens. The key here is obvious—only the healthiest specimens will do. The reproductive cycle inflicts great strain on any animal, and only the strong survive. Turtles that are suffering from any kind of illness not only won't give you any breeding results, they also may die. It is strongly advised that all specimens be given some time to

adjust to captivity before they are used as breeding subjects. Spend the extra required time to do it right and the results will be *very* rewarding.

Other factors are kind of obvious. The males and females must of course be of breeding age (with some female maps this can

Only the finest-quality specimens should be considered for a captive-breeding program. The hibernation term in particular is a great strain on a captive turtle, and unhealthy specimens probably won't even survive it.

be very old indeed). Telling males from females isn't terribly difficult. Adult males almost always are considerably smaller than adult females. Also, females tend to have flat plastrons whereas those of the males are concave. Males usually have longer front claws than females, and the tail also is a bit longer. Finally, the cloacal opening on males usually is a bit farther from the plastron than that of the females.

PREPARATIONS FOR HIBERNATION

The turtles discussed in this book generally hibernate underwater, more particularly in the silty, muddy bottoms of creeks, lakes, and so on. Sometimes they will wedge themselves between rocks or in submerged tree stumps.

The thermoregulation of many aquatic turtles is a fascinating topic all its own and much too detailed to discuss at any

PHOTO OF AN ORNATE DIAMONDBACK TERRAPIN, *MALACLEMYS TERRAPIN MACROSPILOTA*, BY PAUL FREED.

Belly of a young Ornate Diamondback Terrapin, *Malaclemys terrapin macrospilota.* **Purchasing your breeder turtles just when they've reached breeder age is ideal.**

PHOTO BY ISABELLE FRANCAIS.

Belly of an Alabama Map Turtle, *Graptemys pulchra*. Don't be afraid to carefully inspect every inch of a turtle that you're thinking of buying for a propagation program. Remember, unhealthy specimens won't breed, so only choose the best.

valuable length in a "keeper's guide" such as this. Along similar lines, it is interesting to note how an aquatic turtle can survive underwater, even with a reduced metabolism, for months at a time. Nevertheless, that's what maps and Diamondbacks do, so, in captivity, you have to provide the proper environment in which they can replicate this behavior.

The first step, before you do anything else, is to clean out the turtles' systems. This means making sure all fecal matter has been removed, because a hibernating turtle with residual fecal matter may die. Two weeks before hibernation, stop feeding the turtles. Then, during the last week, let them bathe in warm water for about three to four hours every day. This will help loosen up remaining waste matter, emptying out the intestinal tract in the process.

The next step is to prepare the hibernaculum. This is where a bit of space is required. Since sexually mature maps and Diamondbacks are pretty large, you're going to need a pretty large container in which to hibernate them. Most people's first thought would be to use a large glass aquarium. I suppose that would be acceptable, but even better is a large watering trough, the kind used with horses. These can be purchased at virtually any feed store (or other farming-supply type outlet). You don't need one that's *enormous*—the model I used to use held, I think, 50-gallons. It was somewhere in the 50s (perhaps it was 55). In any case, it did the job. They sell 110-gallon models, and even some that are larger. If you have a lot of turtles to hibernate, perhaps you'll want one this size.

Whatever container you decide to use, it must of course be leak-proof. Cover the bottom with about 10 in/25.4 cm of soil (or an 80/20 mixture of soil and sand), then fill it with water until the water level

Keepers should make a point of breeding the more uncommon map turtles or Diamondback Terrapins, like this Alabama Map Turtle, *Graptemys pulchra*. Most forms are swiftly losing their stability in the wild.

PHOTO BY K. H. SWITAK.

PHOTO BY R. D. BARTLETT.

Before trying to breed any of the rarer map turtles or Diamondback Terrapins, perhaps you should start off with some of the more common forms. The Mississippi Map Turtle, *Graptemys pseudogeographica kohni*, for example, has been bred and raised through many generations and is quite common in the herp hobby.

PHOTO OF AN ORNATE DIAMONDBACK TERRAPIN, *MALACLEMYS TERRAPIN MACROSPILOTA*, BY JIM MERLI.

Make sure any specimens slated for hibernation are completely "cleaned out" (i.e., do not have any remaining fecal matter in their systems) before their ambient temperature is lowered. Extraneous fecal matter in the gut of a hibernating turtle will ferment and damage the intestinal walls, probably killing the animal in the process.

is about six inches above the "mud." Beyond that, all you really need to do is place some kind of covering over the top for security purposes (like a sheet of plywood with a large hole cut in the center and covered with some screening).

THE HIBERNATION PERIOD

Now that you've got the hibernaculum set up and the turtles prepared, it's time to begin the hibernation period. As you may know, one of the keys to hibernation is a low temperature. This allows the a turtle's

Lower the turtles' ambient temperature *slowly*. Don't just take them from an 80°F/26°C enclosure and let them loose in cold water. You'll shock the daylights out of them (you might kill them). Allow the temperature to drop about five degrees per day until you reach the ideal temperature of about 52°F/11°C. The water temperature in the hibernaculum should be about 45 to 50°F/7 to 10°C. Once the surroundings have reached these magical numbers, gently place the turtles into the hibernaculum and let them burrow in. Don't disturb

PHOTO BY W. P. MARA.

Young map turtles and Diamondback Terrapins, like this year-old Ornate Diamondback Terrapin, *Malaclemys terrapin macrospilota*, don't need to be hibernated since they aren't going to be used as breeders until they are sexually mature.

metabolism to slow and its body to rest, giving the sexual hormones a chance to sort of "recharge." If hibernation does not occur, your turtles may still breed, but chances are no eggs will be produced.

them while they're hibernating, and don't let the water temperature grow too warm or else the turtles may snap out of their torpor and begin swimming around (Diamondbacks are particularly

BOTH PHOTOS BY W. P. MARA.

Every now and then, a "freak" animal will turn up in a litter. This Mississippi Map Turtle, *Graptemys pseudogeographica kohni*, for example, has light reddish orange striping on the head (making it of the "pastel" variety) and a slightly distorted belly pattern. Animals like this are quite rare and often become the lynchpin of selective breeding programs.

sensitive to sudden warm spells). Also, leave the hibernaculum in darkness and in quiet. In short, *don't disturb hibernating turtles.* You should check on them only when trying to ascertain their state of well-being. If any specimens are losing weight rapidly or showing other signs of severe hibernation stress, remove them immediately, warm them back up, and get them back into a

MATING TIME

Once the hibernation period is complete, the turtles can be taken out of their hibernaculum and placed back into their normal, active-season quarters. Again, raise their ambient temperature slowly, then give them a day or two to reorient themselves. By the third or fourth day, try offering food. Once they start eating again, mating can begin.

If the turtles' setup is housed in

Newborn maps and Diamondbacks can be hibernated in spite of the fact that they can't be used as breeders the following season. However, the mortality rate among newborns in hibernation can be quite high, so the risk really is not worthwhile. Shown is a normally colored Mississippi Map Turtle, *Graptemys pseudogeographica kohni*.

regular feeding cycle.

A sensible and effective hibernation period should last from two to three months. That's close enough to their term in the wild and will effect the desired sexual stimuli.

a large glass aquarium, let them breed there. If the enclosure isn't particularly large, empty out the hibernaculum container and use that. Fill it with about six inches of water, and be sure to include a large land body.

Once the males get "in the mood," they will approach the females and may perform some odd courtship rituals. They may stroke the female's face, swim in circles around her, nudge her, things like that. These actions simply are attempts to get her aroused. Once he thinks his prospective mate is interested, he will mount her from behind and attempt to wrap his tail around hers. If she is receptive, copulation will commence, lasting around 15 to 30

CARE OF THE GRAVID FEMALE

Once a few matings have been observed, you should put the female in her own setup and continue feeding her as usual. Sometimes a gravid female will refuse food, but this is normal. If she appears to be losing weight at a rapid rate, bring her to a vet; if not, don't worry about it. If, on the other hand, her appetite does not decrease, give her a little more nutrition than usual. She will, after all, be carrying eggs, all of which need their own nourishment.

PHOTO BY K. H. SWITAK.

Unless it is absolutely necessary, gravid female turtles should *not* be handled. Undue stress can cause a female to lay her clutch prematurely, and then the eggs, obviously, will not hatch. Shown is a Mangrove Diamondback Terrapin, *Malaclemys terrapin rhizophorarum.*

minutes. Once completed, the female(s) should be removed and placed in a separate enclosure, then introduced again a few days because repeated breedings will ensure successful fertilization.

Also, you may notice a gravid female basking more often than usual. This too is normal. She is warming herself to encourage proper egg production. To aid her during this time, you might want to slightly increase the

The ideal bedding for incubating turtle eggs either is vermiculite, sphagnum moss, or a combination of both (as shown here). Remember to keep the bedding moist, but don't let it get soggy.

temperature at her basking site. Length of gestation for maps and Diamondbacks varies highly, but a general time of between two to three months is about right.

NESTING/EGGLAYING

When the time to lay eggs draws near, a keeper must provide the mother with a nesting spot. This, in essence, means a large land area with a soft substrate. For map turtles, a slightly moistened soil bedding works well. For Diamondbacks, a mixture of sand and soil (80/20), slightly moistened, will do nicely. The mother will dig a burrow and lay her eggs, the whole process taking about 30 minutes to an hour. Do not disturb her during this time. Once she drops her pile, she'll make some attempt to cover it and then walk away, her parental duties completed.

EGG INCUBATION

Once the eggs have been laid, it is advised you incubate them somewhere other than in the burrow dug out by the mother. An effective incubation container can be made from a plastic shoebox or sweaterbox (depending on how much space you need), filled with a 3-in/7.6-cm layer of moistened vermiculite. The top of the container should have some small holes drilled through it, but not so many that all the moisture in the "incubator" is allowed to escape. Vermiculite is a moisture-retaining medium that can be purchased at most any gardener's supply store. Sphagnum moss also works well, but with turtle eggs I have found the vermiculite to be a little better. Some keepers prefer to use a combination of the two, using the vermiculite as a base and the sphagnum moss as a "draping" over the exposed parts of the eggs.

Once you've got the container all set up, you have to place in the eggs. *Carefully* remove them from the burrow and bury them halfway into the vermiculite. Keep in mind that *they must remain in the exact position in which they were laid.* Turtle eggs that have been turned almost always spoil. To keep track of which end is "up," simply mark the top of the egg with a water-based magic marker.

Do not allow the substrate in the incubation container to dry out; this undoubtedly will destroy the eggs. Use your finger or, even better, a soil hygrometer (also available at many garden shops), to determine when the substrate needs to be "watered." A spray bottle will aid you in this endeavor, as will a light trickle of water around inside of the container. Do not allow the eggs themselves to get wet, for this may spoil them.

HATCHING/CARE OF YOUNG

If all goes well, the turtle eggs should hatch in about 70 to 130 days, depending on temperature and the species in question. Once the young have cut through their shells and poked their noses out, they may decide to remain inside for a day or two. Let them. Don't force them to come out until they're good and ready.

PHOTOS BY MELLA PANZELLA (TOP) AND R. D. BARTLETT (BOTTOM).

Hatchling map turtles and Diamondback Terrapins must be given a large water body, but they also must have an area of dry land that is *easy to climb onto*. Also, they will be very active and aggressive and thus will need to eat every day. Finally, the provision of full-spectrum lighting is crucial during their first two to three years. Shown are hatchling Diamondback Terrapins.

A simple incubation container—a bedding of both vermiculite and sphagnum moss covers the floor of an opaque plastic shoebox. The top, not shown, has about a dozen small holes drilled through it for ventilation purposes.

You've waited this long, you can wait a little longer.

Once they do come out, you'll notice a small, almost gross-looking sac stuck to their bellies. This is the embryonic

A herpetoculturist's greatest prize—a healthy, captive-bred neonate. In this case, the animal is a Mangrove Diamondback Terrapin, *Malaclemys terrapin rhizophorarum.*

yolk sac, and it should be left alone. In time it will dry up and fall off, leaving a crack/scar behind, which also will heal. Also, a neonate's shell will feel quite soft, but don't let this alarm you. It's perfectly normal.

The newborns should be placed in their own enclosure (with a large and accessible land body) and offered everything you can think of until an effective feeding regimen is determined. They will grow quickly and need plenty of nutrition, not to mention a generous helping of full-spectrum lighting. It is during the first year or two that their shells will be at their most crucial developmental stage, and deprivation of calcium will cause deformities. Again, give them plenty of food (with an occasional vitamin supplement and full-spectrum light.